# MY
# LOVE AFFAIR
## WITH AN
# ALIEN

Charleston, SC
www.PalmettoPublishing.com

*My Love Affair with an Alien*
Copyright © 2023 by Laura Knighton Curtis

Paperback ISBN: 979-8-8229-2538-0

# MY
# LOVE AFFAIR
## WITH AN
# ALIEN

### AND A LITTLE TOWN CALLED ROSWELL

## LAURA KNIGHTON CURTIS

This book is dedicated to my children: Madison, Bramlett, Kennedy, and Gable. They have dropped everything in their lives time and time again just to go explore Roswell with me and to be with me while my broken heart mended. I am so thankful for them. This book is also dedicated to my father, who has always taken the time to discuss aliens and to listen to me talk about Roswell. We both believe aliens are out there, and they really do exist. Like Dad says, "They are in the Bible, just read it for yourself." Thank you, Dad, for teaching me to "look it up," always, instead of just giving me the answer. Mom, and Lydia, thank you for putting up with me. Finn and Raven, Momo loves you so much. Thank you, guys, for everything. I love you.

*"We're all a little broken somehow. All we can hope to find in this life is that person who gathers and protects all of our broken pieces until we're ready to heal."*
—Miles

# Foreword

This little town has given me many fond memories and adventures. In this place, you can often find people dressed as aliens at least one weekend out of the year, if not every day of the year. If you have not been to Roswell in July, you do not know what you are missing. This book is my way of showing how wonderful the stores, people, and courthouse lawn where they hold festivals are. It is also my way of showing gratitude to my children, who have traveled sixteen hours or more to see this little town just one more time. I'm going to attempt in the chapters of this little book to show you some of the joys that I have found in this wonderful town. Friendly people, a wonderful museum, and lots of unique shops can be found here. If I can give Roswell one-quarter of the justice it deserves, you will understand why I fell in love with Roswell. Sit down, pour yourself a glass of wine—or whatever beverage you like—and get ready to hear about the trip of a lifetime. Then, once you have read my book, pack your suitcase and head out to see it for yourself.

# Table of Contents

# The Cover That Almost Was

When I started writing this book, I asked Gable to create the cover for me. He drew it on lined paper, and since he is a high school senior, works full time, and is in theatre and show choir, he remains quite busy. My children are such a big part of my life (really, they are my everything), so I wanted them to participate by not only going to Roswell over and over but by being part of this project. Gable participated by drawing, and Madison participated in words. Here, in Madison's words, are her thoughts on Roswell:

Roswell...the town I never knew I needed to land in. I've lost count of how many times I've crashed there thanks to my mom. A trip to alien country always brings us closer together than we were before. It has a way of getting us to look at hard truths and take off any and all blinders in order to ask ourselves the deeper questions we tend to answer on autopilot. Whether we hear an unwelcome sound at Bottomless Lakes State Park around three in the morning followed by green streaks in the sky, or both dress like aliens just to dance the night away in downtown Roswell with robots on stilts, we always have the time of our lives. The atmosphere brings childlike fun out in all of us. You leave there feeling like you've gained a whole new home with happy-hearted souls in every quaint shop and restaurant. On the surface, it may seem like a town to visit if you're one for conspiracies. On the contrary. It's one of the best places for the whole family. I swear, there is something there for everyone. Ever dream of eating a Big Mac in a spaceship where the ice cream machine actually works? Ever tried authentic Mexican green chili? In the mood for a classy winery and live music? Or maybe you just want to take a stroll with your dog and let the aliens and space murals fascinate you everywhere you look? Bring your fur babies and stay at the Roswell Inn! Take selfies in front of all the aliens and, like us, unexpectedly leave a piece of your heart there.

Before visiting Roswell, New Mexico, I thought aliens were something to fear—I didn't want to mess with them, and I certainly didn't want them coming near me. I was scared to believe. Somehow that fear has shifted into friendly respect. Just like most of us have experienced some misunderstandings in our lives, we can imagine what alien life has been treated like when discovered. We all see how people can shun and abuse humans that look and think more uniquely than the majority. The people of Roswell teach us that there is another way. We can celebrate differences and lean into the excitement of learning from what we don't yet understand. I'll be back to bring in more Fourth of Julys at their annual UFO festival, and I hope to see you there too!

—An alien lover's daughter, Madison MonRoe Curtis

# The Day My Ex-Husband Was Abducted by the Men in Black

I thought I should tell you a little about myself before getting to my love affair with an alien. I, Laura Curtis, was married to Paul Kevin Curtis for ten years and had four beautiful children with him. We divorced but continued to raise our children as best we could, when we were not arguing. In April of 2013, I got a call from the FBI saying my ex-husband, who had been en route to my house, would not be coming. It got worse. They had arrested my ex-husband for trying to kill the president of the United States, and possibly for the bombing at the Boston Marathon, and potentially for shooting an elephant at the Barnum & Bailey Circus in Tupelo, Mississippi. They said they were coming to interview me and to search my house for traces of ricin. It seems that Kevin, as I call him, had possibly created ricin and sent it to President Obama, along with a judge, a prosecutor, and a state senator. I have to tell you, I thought it was a joke. I just ignored the call and sat there, until it hit me: they said "en route." Who says "en route" except FBI men, or the infamous men in black? About that time, I looked on the television and saw breaking news that Paul Kevin Curtis had been arrested for trying to kill the president. I thought, Uh-oh. So first things first. Due to the fact I lived in a dry county, and I had quite a collection of wine, I grabbed every kid I could find to haul my wine out to the ditch and hide it. Then I sat down trying to look like a perfectly law-abiding citizen and just waited for the FBI.

I spent the next few hours dealing with the FBI and learning that my ex-husband had been taken to Oxford, Mississippi, to be held in the federal prison. They asked me thousands of questions, including whether I thought he had the capability and mentality to make ricin. I said no. I said Kevin couldn't make a cake without blowing up the oven. Finally they left, and I thought it was over. The kids and I brought all the wine back in and set it back in the kitchen and went to bed. The next day, while I was at college studying criminal justice, emphasis on homeland security—funny, right?—I get a call in class, and it's the FBI wanting to come search my house. I am like, sure, I'll meet you there. Then it hit me. I had all this wine back in my house. I racked my brain on what to do and thought, what else can I do but be honest? So, I call the FBI guy back, and when he answered, I said, "Uh, I have a problem." He's like, "What?" I said, "Well, I have something in my house that is illegal, and I hid it last night, but I put it back." He went, "Really?" I said, "Yes, I have a whole bunch of wine, and this is a dry county." All I could think of was that my children's parents were both about to be in jail, their father for ricin and me for wine. When I mentioned wine, he broke out laughing. He said, "I thought you were confessing to ricin. I don't give a crap about wine."

One other thing about the strong, vivacious men in black. They are afraid of ferrets. When they began to search my house, I mentioned I had a ferret that hung loose in the house, and his name was Clyde. One looked at the other and said, "I am scared of those things," and the other said, "I am not going back there. Those things bite." The one looked at me and said, "Secure the ferret, ma'am!" So off I went and found him. I brought him out and showed the men, and they backed away saying, "Put him away!" True story.

The last story is about the fact that my ex-husband, Kevin, is writing a book about body parts, because he claimed the local hospital was selling body parts. The FBI knew this, because they had confiscated his computers and writing material the night before. Well, the one agent climbed up in the attic to look around, and when he opened the attic door, a foot from our Halloween decorations fell out and bounced down the stairs. I swear that agent screamed like a girl. The other agent laughed and laughed. To hear more about these stories and more about Kevin being framed, you can watch the documentary called *The Kings of Tupelo*. My ex-husband is an Elvis impersonator, and the guy that actually framed him is a karate instructor. It started with a battle between them over who was the best singer and the best at karate. It really is a funny story. Trying to prove Kevin's innocence and get him out of jail actually drew us closer together as a family.

My life has not been easy as a single mom of four kids with an ex-husband like Kevin, and then a fiancé who jilted me on Valentine's Day several years later, but I would not have wanted a different life. My kids are my rocks, and my forever sidekicks. With them by my side, I have learned that I am strong. I believe in God, and I know He put me where I am today, and I love every minute of life. Now that you know a little more about me, let's get to aliens and Roswell, the town that I have fallen in love with! As Paul Harvey used to say, "Here is the rest of the story."

# Chasing William Shatner

My love affair with Roswell began in the summer of 2017. It was an incredibly hot day in early August. The air-conditioning barely helped to keep the car halfway cool, and I was thirsty for a cold drink. I was on the way to Las Vegas to a *Star Trek* convention with my fiancé, and we decided to pull over at a gas station that had appeared suddenly on our horizon. What happened next would change my life.

I straightened my stiff body and got out of the car and walked into the old gas station. I walked over to the refrigerated section and opened the doors and paused for a minute to let the cold air hit my body and cool me off. I grabbed an icy Coke and put it against my forehead. It had been a quiet few hours in the car with my fiancé since we had not been speaking due to an argument we'd had that morning. Eager to talk to someone, I started a conversation with the cashier. She was a friendly type, and asked where we were traveling to. When I told her I was going to my first *Star Trek* convention to meet William Shatner, she said, "Since you're this close, you need to drive through Roswell." I immediately perked up and asked, "*The* Roswell?" My fiancé (whom I shall call Fido for the rest of this book) hurried over to join this conversation and said, "We are not going to Roswell. We don't have time and it's six hours out of the way!" I looked at him and said, "We are going to Roswell!"

We continued to argue as my fiancé and I climbed back into the car to travel toward Las Vegas. Fido said, "Our tires are already bad, they're barely going to make it to Las Vegas. We are not going six hours out of the way." I begged, "Please, I have wanted to go to Roswell my entire life!" The funny thing was, I didn't even know I had wanted to go to Roswell until I heard the woman in the gas station comment that Roswell was nearby. In that moment, I knew in my subconscious that I had dreamed about going to this place for years. We managed to strike up a deal. We would go to Roswell, buy tires, spend two hours there while mechanics put the tires on my vehicle, and then we would head on to William Shatner and Vegas.

# Are You a Believer?

We pulled into a tire place called Discount Tires of Roswell and left my vehicle with these nice people that were actual Roswell citizens. I was filled with excitement to be in this little town. We walked around, saw what we could, and when the car was ready, we headed down to the center of town and discovered this amazing building called the International UFO Museum and Research Center. We pulled over, went inside, and found out that for five dollars we could see a lot of information about UFOs. This nice man asked if we were in the military, and since Fido had been a marine, he got in for two dollars. When he gave us our tickets, the man at the front desk asked, "Are you a believer?" We both said yes. He then said these words: "Well, if you're not, you will be when you leave." I found out later that this man was Dennis Balthasar. I will never forget those words he spoke to me that afternoon. They would have an impact on my entire life.

As I walked in, having always been a speed reader, I hungrily absorbed every article on the walls inside this little museum. I read every document from Roswell citizens in 1947 and in the years afterward that had been notarized. I looked at every piece of evidence, proof, and theory, and breathed it all into my body for the next hour. I saw the displays. I saw evidence from the men in black who had sent letters to witnesses that had seen things, and to some who had heard things from witnesses of the UFO crash. I saw a comment where someone said that Mac Brazel, who never had two nickels to rub together, went off with men in black from the government after the crash, and he returned with a new truck and was able to start a business. All of this made me ponder. I kept pondering in my mind on these facts as we drove to Las Vegas. I turned to Fido and said I'm going back there and doing more research, and I'm bringing my children back there one day. In those two hours, I had fallen in love with this little town. It had spoken to me as no other town had ever spoken to me in my entire life. Fido said, "This is a once in a lifetime trip." I said, "It may be for you, but not for me." Little did I know, this was one of the most truthful statements I had ever made.

# You Fell in Love for a Weekend

### (But I Fell in Love for the Rest of My Life)

Let's fast-forward to a year and a half later. Fido, in 2019 on Valentine's Day, decided to break up with me after almost six years of being together and three years of being engaged. While eating at a Mexican restaurant, he hands me a Pandora bracelet and says, "I am going to see other women." I looked at the bracelet and the only charm on it was a heart. On it, the heart said, "Follow your heart." A big question for me has always been, how do you know where your heart lies, when you have so many people that you love? How do you choose what means the most to your heart? Over the next few months, I would figure out what my heart's desires were and begin to follow them. As I drove home after Fido broke up with me, I cried and pondered my life. My heart was broken, and I went home to my children and continued crying for the next couple of months. All four kids were there for me and put their arms around me, but after a couple of months they began to be a little tired of hearing me cry. The same could be said for my coworkers. I had to rethink my life and change the future goals that I had, where I was going to marry this man and travel in a camper around the United States. To help reestablish my life and my dreams, I began to think of Roswell. I actually had never stopped thinking of Roswell, but somehow, I knew this little town could help heal my heart. I went to some of my children and asked, "Will you go to Roswell with me in July? I want to show you this town that I've fallen in love with and let you fall in love with it for yourselves." They agreed to go, and on July 4, 2019, we started out for the big little town of Roswell.

As we were traveling, I started googling about the town to show my kids and build their excitement and, lo and behold, to my amazement, I found out Roswell was having a UFO festival this exact weekend! I shared this with my children and told them we've got to stop and buy alien costumes! We spent the night in Amarillo, Texas, went to a darling little costume shop downtown and purchased our alien outfits and makeup, and headed out the next day to Roswell to join the other alien chasers at the 2019 UFO Festival. But, before we headed on, we had to try out The Big Texan Steak Ranch in Amarillo to eat steak and drink their amazing homemade beer. We took selfies in their jail cell setup, we ate their amazing desserts, played shooting games, and listened to music. If you have ever seen *King of the Hill* and watched the episode where Bobby is determined to eat a 72-ounce steak at a restaurant in Amarillo, this is the restaurant. If you can eat a 72-ounce steak in an hour, along with all the fixings, you get the meal for free. Let's just say that none of us attempted to do this. After indulging in food and sleep, we headed on to the festival.

The UFO festival had turned this little sleepy town into a sizzling, exciting, and busy weekend destination. I was so grateful to have seen the town of Roswell when it wasn't festival time. It allowed me to fall in love with the people and the little businesses without seeing all the festival activities. But I digress.

During the festival, my son Gable and I decided to get some ice cream and we went into a little ice cream place where aliens were displayed all over the walls, like in every other business in Roswell. Again, to remind you, I was just getting over a broken romance, and I had told my children we could not listen to any sad or romantic music on the entire trip. So, while I was buying a milk shake and some ice cream for my little boy, a song comes over the speaker and I heard these words, "You fell in love for a weekend, but I fell in love for the rest of my life." I burst into tears and just started crying and the woman at the ice cream counter asked, "Are you OK?" I nodded, my son grabbed my hand, and we went and sat down at this little table next to an alien statue. A few minutes later, my daughter came along decked out in an alien costume and her dog, Willow, had her UFO costume on. I looked at them and my heart healed just a little bit in that moment. If any of you have suffered a lost love, you will understand the loss my heart and mind was feeling at this time, but the sight of my daughter, who loved me enough to not only drive thousands of miles by my side, but also was willing to dress her and her precious doggy, as aliens made me realize love comes in many forms.

What I have learned from this little town is that, when I was aching and hurting inside, it took those feelings and gave me some peace and excitement so that I could march on and continue on to a better life, a different life not filled with sadness. As I thought more about my life and the fascination I felt toward this town, I realized that this song that tore my heart out really was not about Fido, it was, in retrospect, about something much bigger. These travelers that were here for a weekend had fallen in love for a weekend of fun and festivities, but I had fallen in love for a lifetime with a town that somehow knew what I needed to move on.

# My Own UFO Sighting

We were fortunate enough to camp in this place called Bottomless Lakes State Park right outside of Roswell. My daughter Madison chose to sleep in the car with her then boyfriend, but my son Gable and I decided to camp in our tent so we could see the stars. We met a couple of people that let us share their wonderful dinner with them. As happens a lot of times in the West, there was a fire ban that weekend. John and his girlfriend had a propane cookstove and they invited us to a meal that was equivalent to a Thanksgiving dinner. After the many hot dogs that we had shared along the trip, it seemed like Thanksgiving dinner to us. We stayed up late talking to these wonderful people. One thing about Roswell, you will not meet a stranger. You can be sitting on a park bench and someone will sit down and offer you a bottle of water because you seem thirsty. I've never gone away caring for people in a town like this before. They have patriotism that fills your heart with gladness to be an American. There is an overall glow of friendship and patriotism that you will find in no other town.

Back to this night—we went to bed late, and as I climbed into the tent with my son, I said good night to my daughter. I went to sleep, but at about four o'clock in the morning, I woke up hearing Willow, Madison's dog, growling like crazy. Willow was outside the car growling at some unseen object. Madison started screaming at her to get in the car and I heard a constant, loud humming noise. I looked out the side of my tent window and saw two bright green neon streaks go straight up to the skies—and that's it. It was gone in a brief period, less than a second. I got chill bumps all over and had a fear that this was so unrealistic and unreasonable. I thought, Why did I decide to camp in Roswell? What was I thinking? Well, I thought surely it was just lightning. It had to be sheets or streaks of lightning, even though I hadn't seen any that green before. And they were swift and side by side, like when a rocket ship streaks out of sight.

I sat for the next hour looking at the spot and looking at the sky, but no lightning appeared. There was no thunder, no humming noise, nothing. I realized the humming had stopped long ago. I finally lay down and went to sleep, but the next morning when Madison and I started getting ready we kept looking at each other. All of a sudden we burst out at the same time, "Mom! Madison! I think I saw a UFO!" We began talking and discovered we both had the same experience. We went and talked to John, a fellow camper nearby that we had met the night before. John said, "I heard the humming noise, and I think it was just the air-conditioning at the bathroom." I asked, "How come we don't hear it now?" Neither he nor we could answer that.

Madison and I decided to keep quiet about it for a couple of years because, after all, no one would believe us. But the more I considered what I saw and thought about at that moment, I knew this was what I saw: just the streak of light in the middle of nowhere, in the Bottomless Lakes State Park with the stars all around. Nothing else was around, nothing but two bright green lights that shot away into the sky in the twinkling of an eye. In my research about UFOs, I find quite a few appear around the Fourth of July. Roswell is the most famous one, but if you just google UFO sightings in July, you will find quite a few. Also, this was right after Fourth of July week in Roswell, the anniversary of the most famous UFO sighting ever. All I could think of was, I have lost my mind for staying around Roswell in July.

# A Misunderstood City's Podcast

One day I was driving along and searching for a new podcast and this podcast came up from nowhere. Kyle Bullock, a local businessman in the city of Roswell, had created a podcast about Roswell. Well, you can imagine I was more than excited! I began listening to this podcast, falling in love with this town all over again! Kyle talked about his hometown and how his grandfather and father had grown up there, and he talked about his jewelry store that had been family owned for generations. I had actually walked by this local business twice when I went to Roswell! I promptly bought his podcast merchandise, fell in love with the story he was telling, and couldn't wait to get in the car to drive to work so I could listen to it more. I ordered this little medallion that he had made for his listeners and put it on my Pandora bracelet. When it fell off somewhere along the way and I lost it, I was heartbroken. I emailed Kyle but he was not making them anymore. One day I told myself I was going to buy a pair of gorgeous earrings from the store. Kyle kindly answered my emails, which proved even more to me that this town is full of kind people. They love their town, and they love people.

I actually cried when he ended his podcast. I emailed him and begged for more about his hometown. Much to my surprise he added another episode a year later, and I felt like when a favorite author writes another book to add to a much-loved series. If you only listen to one podcast in your lifetime, listen to Kyle Bullock's *Crashed in Roswell: Survivors in a Misunderstood City*. I feel God has used this town, this podcast, and the UFO festivals celebrated yearly to help mend my broken heart and give me hope for my future. I won't be alone just by myself. I can go to this town and be swept along into the local businesses, volunteer alongside everyone else and decorate for Christmas and Easter and the UFO festivals, and go to Chile Cheese festivals and to every courthouse lawn celebration. My older years won't be alone but be filled with the excitement of seeing this town year after year. I follow Roswell on Facebook and watch its citizens come together to decorate for every season. Then, I watch them all come together to take down the decorations. They plant flowers together as a community, sell fresh vegetables on the courthouse lawn on summer weekends, and gather for parades for Memorial Day and Veterans Day. I have never seen such a patriotic, America-loving town in my life. It brings me back to my Ronald Reagan years every time I witness these events. Roswell is proud of their veterans and of our American flag. If you find yourself missing patriotism, just go visit on one of these weekends and you will feel yourself swelling with pride for our country.

# The Festival That Never Was

It was 2020, need I say more? After so much fun at the 2019 UFO Festival, I couldn't wait till 2020 came around so I could go to the festival once more. I was on a roll. Then 2020 and COVID happened. Then nothing happened. I whined along with everyone else about everything being canceled. When I found out shirts were going to be made for the festival that never was, I did what I could to help do my part in supporting this little town and bought the shirt. I wore it to the 2021 UFO Festival, and I wore it proudly. I felt bad for Roswell. I knew businesses depended on this festival to make it through the rest of the year. The 2020 festival went on for its local residents, but crowds were frowned on. The show did go on and I watched it on Facebook, but believe me guys, this is not the same. But, on the bright side, this only helped to build suspense for the upcoming biggest anniversary of all: seventy-five years of history to celebrate!

If you have never been to a UFO Festival, let me tell you a little about it. My personal favorite part of the festival is at night. Fellow alien lovers enjoy many hours and days of parades, shopping, movies, alien runs, human costume contests, and animal costume contests. At night, we head to the green-domed courthouse and the lawn. Men on stilts, dancers covered in lights, and entertainers singing patriotic and popular songs can mesmerize one for hours. Young and old alike get to their feet and dance the night away. The ones that can't stand will clap and sway and smile to the music. A mixture of magic and patriotic emotions rush over one as the night goes on. Ten-foot-tall robot dancers give glow sticks to enthusiastic festival goers who wave them in the air. Roswell festival nights—if you surrender yourself to them—can be magical. When the 2021 UFO festival was announced, this Roswell fan had already booked her room for the Roswell Inn. I was finally going to take all my four kids to Roswell, the UFO festival, and the International UFO Museum.

# Are We There Yet?

### June 30, 2021,

We headed out in the middle of the night to Roswell—me, four kids, Madison's boyfriend, Tara (my son Kennedy's bride-to-be), and three dogs—all stuffed into two cars. Two days, five states, and one big vet bill in Amarillo later (due to one dog coming down with parvovirus on the way), we finally arrived in Roswell. The bad news? We missed the registration deadline for the animal contest, and all the bribing in the world didn't help. Picture my Labradoodle wearing a silver cape, Reynolds aluminum-wrapped antennas, and silver boots. I just know he would have won! I think they felt so sorry for me that they put him on the front page of their website for the festival. Check it out! I think it is still on their Facebook page. The good news was that Appa, the Great Pyrenees, made a full recovery from parvovirus!

As usual, we stayed in the Roswell Inn, one of my personal favorite hotels. Unfortunately, there were five of us and three dogs all stuffed into one room. We watched the parade and went to a free, Fourth of July 4 Creedence Clear Creek fan music concert that included a light show you needed to be there to believe. My kids got to see the International UFO Museum and spend two hours exploring and taking pictures and selfies. I chose to watch the documentary where witnesses from six decades told their stories. My favorite part was dancing the night away, with dogs and all. Ten-foot-tall men and women wearing lights danced on stilts along with us.

If you have never been to a Roswell UFO festival, make sure you stay till the last hour of the last night. Picture children laughing and waving light sticks, dogs in costumes, and funnel cakes on the courthouse lawn. Old and young alike laugh and smile at the costumes and music. Everyone is generous with their compliments for each other's costumes and their cute animals. Right down the street, in walking distance, is a very unusual McDonald's. It's the only McDonald's in the world that is like this one. It is shaped like, wait for it…a UFO. There are alien statues inside and out. The inside is shaped like a UFO too. On one of our visits, we had our dog with us. We snuck him in under the table, and since he was dressed in an alien outfit no one seemed to care. The ice cream machine even works!  If anyone has ever lived in the South,  quite often you will find McDonald's ice cream machine being shut down for service. I can not count the times my children and I have stopped for a milk shake, and here these words, "I am sorry, our ice-cream machine is down". Therefore , you can imagine our excitement to be able to get ice cream! Some people have driven across the country just for this unusual fast-food place, and when you take in the whole experience of eating a hamburger in a UFO while wearing an alien costume, you're on cloud nine, literally.

# Sharon's Story of Her Own UFO Sighting

In this chapter I will tell you about a relative of mine who has had her own UFO sightings. My cousin Sharon sent me this a few years ago out of the blue because she had to tell somebody. This is her story in her own words.

"I was in a deaf camp in Murfreesboro, Tennessee, with some church kids (our parents thought we needed some humility), and we were the *only* group that *was not* deaf! Just the conversation hums alone were terrifying! Just think about that for a second.

"Well, it was strange to me every second. When I was lying in my top bunk bed looking up at the stars and trees—there was only wood frame and netting in our sleeping quarters—and feeling so homesick for anywhere but there, I saw an extreme brightness in the sky. As it grew closer…there was no sound whatsoever. I thought, 'Jesus Christ himself is coming to take me.' I was ready. To my shock and complete peace, there was a huge round object just above the trees and it was *completely* silent!

"I saw a round object about twenty feet wide and maybe ten feet high with a circle of lights on bottom and a smaller circle of lights on top. It passed slowly and the lights were beautiful over the trees. I was very disappointed that they didn't get me (as I believed they came for me in my time of need). I never spoke of that experience until I was in my twenties and only to my two closest friends. I have only told maybe ten people in my life because of the look I always get of 'bitch for-real crazy.' Yes, I've gotten that look maybe all my life, but…I saw it and still to this day have it imprinted in my brain. I'm just waiting for confirmation for *all* the ones who have laughed at me or are surely unbelievers! There is so much info out there, including documentaries and actual TV shows about UFO untold truths with interviews of air force pilots and police. And there are many other stories from around the world. It's all coming out and soon! I will finally be believed! I have issues about the relationship between God's story and aliens but, hey, I *know* they are real and I'm ready for the world to know! And, yes, I may be crazy, but I saw what I saw, crazy as hell or not!"

She continued to talk to me about her experience.

"I thought maybe you had an experience like mine that made you want to go to Roswell. You've missed out on a phenomenal experience, but it mostly opened my eyes to so many what-ifs. I've constantly been looking in the sky since then, hoping for another experience with such an intriguing subject. I am a little worried about their intentions, but, for damn sure, aliens are real!

"I pray it's both and not one and the same! There is just so much relationship between angels, time travel, and demons. It's so confusing, but what I saw brought me the most peaceful and calming energy I ever felt all through my soul! Thanks for not making fun of me. I also have been an *extreme* Prince fan since age thirteen, and my UFO experience was at about ten or eleven. I got the *same* damn reaction when I told people about my lifetime love of Prince—laughs and anti-gay jokes—but if you *ever* listened to his 'unpopular songs,' you'd get it too! I'll give you one to try: 'The Love We Make.'

"He was a very spiritual person and dedicated his last ten-plus years to writing songs related to 'listen to God, read your Bible,' and that just confirmed my reason to have him touch my soul in such a spiritual, loving way."

Everyone has their own philosophy. Are aliens really demons? Are they fallen angels? Are they from another planet? I continue to research other's beliefs and their personal sightings.

# Get Your Kicks on Route 66

When you are driving sixteen hours to the grand city of Roswell, Route 66 is a must. Whichever way you are driving, you can stumble on that historic highway and make your trip a heartfelt learning experience. On my drive in March to gather more information to finish my book, my daughter and I traveled through Oklahoma City and stopped off at a nostalgic haven for gamers, Flashback RetroPub. Eli, Madison's partner, was gracious enough to let Madison and I to have this girl time, and for Madison to accompany me as my photographer. We spent two delightful hours drinking beer local to Oklahoma and playing Mario Kart, Duck Hunt, Skee-Ball, and other Nintendo games on old-fashioned televisions. The options were never ending. We continued on the next day, taking a slight detour onto Route 66, and stopped off at the Route 66 Museum in Clinton Oklahoma . There, you can learn the history of Route 66, watch a film, and take lots of selfies with vintage items.

When I was a child, my dad always took us on vacations where we learned a little history at the same time. Route 66 is such a huge part of our country, which I never realized until I drove down this route. You can see dinosaur and blue whale sculptures, graffiti-covered Cadillacs, closed-down gas stations, and old signs from mom-and-pop businesses that closed due to the new interstate being built across America. A personal preference is to go through Amarillo and eat at The Big Texan, where you can get a 72-ounce steak for free if you can eat it all. I think you probably are catching on to the fact that I like to eat, especially steak! If you choose to eat a smaller steak, you can pay for and enjoy it at your own leisure.

While you are in Amarillo, you can find the Route 66 Historic District going through downtown. Graffiti art abounds, and nestled among the many local shops I came across a charming gaming store where one can buy rare video games and toys. I know, because I've been there twice. The Cadillac Ranch is just down the route, and there you can pick up a discarded can of spray paint and paint on one of the upright, half-buried cars yourself. My goal is to see Route 66 in every state by the end of my traveling days. If you have a love of history and Americana like I do, you should take yourself, your children, and your significant other and travel down this Route 66—and make sure you stop off at Roswell before you go any farther.

# March 24, 2023, We Landed in Roswell

As I drove into Roswell to finalize my research and finish the book, as usual, I had to catch my breath due to excitement. My daughter Madison and I checked into our usual landing spot, the Roswell Inn, let the dogs take a walk, changed clothes, and headed to a wonderful restaurant called the Cattle Baron. Deborah, a friendly Roswell citizen, was our waitress. She gave us recommendations on what to eat, and her and my personal favorite is the rib eye steak, smothered in pepper and special seasoning. Homemade bread, a glass of wine, and a salad bar loaded with everything imaginable made the meal wonderful and tasty beyond words. I can't even start to describe the salad bar.

We talked to Deborah about the new steak restaurant chain that had come to town and was beginning to hurt their business. As I looked around, I still saw many happy families enjoying a meal out in a classy restaurant. When I have a choice, I will always choose locally owned. These are the dollars that keep a town intact as a village where you live with loved ones and sit around the dinner table at the end of the day. When you get to Roswell, make sure you stop and say hello to Deborah and order that rib eye and glass of wine. There are many wonderful places to eat, but this place is a must. Madison and I took a selfie in front of the Cattle Baron's sign, acting like our normal goofy selves away from everyday problems. Then we climbed into the car so we could enjoy a glass of wine with our baby dogs at the motel.

# Caffeine Galore at Stellar Coffee Co.

If you're like me and my daughter, your first thought in the morning is a cup of coffee. To get that fix, we headed down Main Street and stopped at an out-of-this-world coffee shop called Stellar Coffee Co. There, my daughter and I talked to Thomas, a local who hangs out at the coffee bar. He told us about the Galacticon and different things to do while we are here. As is typical of Roswell citizens, he was friendly, and we carried on conversations while drinking coffee. In the corner were earrings that you can buy, handmade by Cameron. I fell in love with a copper pair that are still calling my name. Unfortunately, someone bought them before I could add them to my collection. Ethan is the friendly barista there who made me a drink that I couldn't describe quite exactly. I can't ever seem to remember those fancy names. During the UFO festival, there will usually be a line out the door, but on a sleepy day in March, my daughter and I had the place to ourselves. Oh, and Stellar Coffee is dog friendly! Almost every place in Roswell is. So if you have a fur baby, make sure you don't leave it behind. They are welcome almost everywhere in Roswell.

# That Perfect Pair of Earrings

My next stop after coffee was to pick out a beautiful pair of earrings at Bullock's Jewelry. Finally! Unique stones embraced by silver had caught my eye on their website, and I had been dreaming about owning a couple of pairs. You know this already if you read my previous chapters. You might realize by now that I do love a pair of earrings, or two or three pairs, or maybe four. This store has a remarkable history and has been in Roswell for ninety-four years now. It is a three-generation family-owned store, and, as I mentioned before, Kyle Bullock, the owner, has a podcast about the town of Roswell. It will keep you listening to the end.

After buying one pair of amethyst earrings, I found another set I just had to have. Red aventurine earrings and a matching necklace were next to the door. I had been studying what these stones can do for one's mental state, so they made their way to my layaway. Angela was my clerk, and she was kind enough to listen as I babbled excitedly about how much I love Roswell. So make one more stop along your way in Roswell if you like fine and unusual jewelry. They can fix you up!

# Museum Time and UFO Books

After I had my cup of coffee and stopped to buy my new earrings, I headed to the International UFO Museum, where I found out that Dennis Balthasar was there for a mini lecture and Q and A session. I promptly bought his book and his DVD about his tour of Roswell. Of course, I was the first one to ask him a question. I had always been curious about why bodies were in one area, but Mac Brazel was in another. Also, how did Jesse Marcel Jr. feel about being a colonel in the army after such a cover-up of the crash? How did Jesse Marcel Sr. feel after being made out to be a fool by the government? My reasoning would be that Marcel Sr. felt he had to have a job, but he also knew the truth, which was enough for him. It's just my opinion, but something to research more for sure.

Every time I come to this museum, I find more evidence that I didn't see the first few times. Zenith, the manager, became a best friend while I was here. Madison and I bought year-long passes for twenty dollars so we can come back anytime we like. The research library provides hours of reading about UFOs and aliens. Every time I come to the museum, I find a new article that I missed before. When you do make it to the museum, make sure you read the witness stories of people that were citizens of Roswell in 1947. Their testimonies were notarized in front of a judge. These testimonies alone led me to believe that just possibly aliens did land here in 1947. Just when I thought I had seen everything, I stumbled into the archives room. Every magazine that has touched on UFOs in the past ten decades has been categorized by year and date here. What a gold mine! In the research library, any report of a UFO Siting, has witnesses listed, possible reasons that it might be a UFO, and gives the explanation and evidence that MUFON lists. MUFON **UFO Network (MUFON)** is a US-based non-profit organization composed of civilian volunteers who study reported UFO sightings. It is one of the oldest and largest organizations of its kind, claiming more than 4,000 members worldwide with chapters and representatives in more than 43 countries and all 50 states, as listed by Wikipedia. What they do, in laymen's term, is take someone's so called siting, and investigate. MUFON checks with the airports, and Government, and will even check with other possible witnesses. When no reason is found other then a unidentified flying object, it is labeled as a UFO. This group takes UFO sightings seriously. They will debunk them in a heartbeat, if they discover a fraudulent claim. So, if you think you see something, don't be shy, call them or email them, and let MUFON do the work. If you have read about a UFO sighting somewhere, you can find any information on it in the Museum's library. I personally have always been interested in the UFO sighting in Zimbabwe. In 1994, 60 children at Ariel school in Ruwa, Zimbabwe said they'd seen a 'UFO' and 'aliens with big eyes' in bush land near their school playground. The story was reported around the world. The story these children told, is quite different. These aren't little grey or green friendly men, they have black hair and are quite scary. I wonder perhaps if this "UFO" might have been from another country, instead of a different Universe. Either way, you will read all information that is available in the International UFO Museum and Research Center, in Roswell New Mexico. They don't call it a Research Center for nothing! Take your cup of coffee in there, and sit a spell, and read to your mind's content.

# Homeless in Roswell

Even in the city of Roswell, you will occasionally find a wanderer without a home. I met a nice young man on a homemade motorcycle with a Chihuahua in his backpack. He proudly pointed out every little part that he had attached and had made into an entire working motorcycle. He told me his story about moving to Roswell in 1994. He said he moved here for a baseball scholarship, but after a year, due to his liking booze and women—his words, not mine—he dropped out of college and his family threw him out. He told me he had been on his own ever since he lost his family due to his addictions, and then he started to cry. I asked, "Is Roswell not like a family to help replace your other family?" He replied, "This town will take care of you if you take care of it. I've stayed here because I have no other place to go but I make it OK." As we parted ways, he shook my hand and said, "I am called Mercy." He rode away and, as he did, that statement about Roswell stayed in my mind. Dorothy at the Cattle Baron told us she took her friend out once a week to do things because she got lonely staying at home. Patty, the owner of Area 52 Tactical Laser Tag, said they moved here because there was nothing to do for the locals. And I listened to Zenith, the manager at the UFO museum, say that this museum is her life, she takes care of the materials in it, and she is proud of what the museum offers. I realized what Mercy said is true: this town really will take care of you if you care about Roswell.

# Mexican Food to Die For

After a day at the International UFO Museum, I was starving. My daughter picked me up and we headed around the corner to eat at Martin's Capitol Café. Michael, our waiter, promptly brought us homemade salsa—that frankly was the best I have ever eaten—partnered with true homemade tortilla chips. I ordered my usual, a fried chimichanga with ground beef. The unusual thing about this restaurant is that they do not fry their chimichangas, but Michael asked me if I would like them fried. I said yes, and when my meal arrived, I proceeded to eat the best chimichanga ever.

You will recall I wrote earlier that I first came to Roswell with my fiancé, Fido. We ate in this restaurant while we were here, and I didn't know how I would handle seeing the same table that Fido and I had sat at and held hands. It took six years to come back to this restaurant, but I was able to do it. I talked to Madison about Fido, and how the green chili salsa was so hot I grabbed and drank his entire beer because my tongue was on fire. I remembered the good times and was able to smile, and to be glad I had those moments. I will always be grateful that he made it possible for me to visit this town. Without Fido, I would have probably never had the chance. This restaurant has bittersweet memories, but I am so glad I got to come back and eat here once again and create updated happy memories to carry with me. When you get to Roswell, make sure you stop by here and get a fried chimichanga. You won't regret it.

# Wine Time

As I sit here in my drunken stupor—I have just enjoyed several delectable glasses of wine at Pecos Flavors Winery & Bistro—I muse about what I will include in this chapter. I listened to jazz music as we drank and ate. I made sure to get a sandwich with green chili on turkey and homemade bread. Living in the south, I can only get authentic green chili when I am visiting Roswell. Ariana, my server, goes simply as Ari. I spent several delightful hours with my daughter at the bar talking to Ari and her daughter, who had stopped by to enjoy lunch and see her mother. My daughter and I felt kinship talking to them, probably because both Ari and I are single moms, and our children are our lives.

Maybe it is the same in other small towns, where you can find friendly people every place you go, but I have begun to think this is just part of Roswell's style. Out front at Pecos Flavors Winery, the usual statue of an alien greets you. I now think that if aliens do choose to come back, they will feel at home here in Roswell. There's Dunkin' Donuts, where a huge alien statue beckons you to come in, and our hotel where an alien is in every corner of the lobby and even on the sign outside. When you do make your journey to Roswell, make sure you stop by and enjoy a glass of wine that's made right here in New Mexico. Say hello to the delightful host who came back home to Roswell to help take care of his mother after being gone for many years, and to Ari at the bar. Also, make sure you pick up a bottle of wine to take home as a souvenir. It might even have an alien on the label to remind you of your trip here. Mine was a special edition sixtieth anniversary bottle of blush wine. That bottle is never going to be opened, but if I change my mind, I'll make a lamp out of it later for sure.

# Laser Tag at Area 52

No trip to Roswell would be complete without visiting Area 52. Yes, I said Area 52. Here, you can enjoy laser tag like no other on fifteen hundred square feet, with plenty of places to hide and military-style weapons to "kill" your fellow enemy. Area 52 Tactical Laser Tag came to be because Patty and her husband decided to retire and move here from Chicago, and they found there was nothing to do at night for Roswell's citizens. They moved here and never looked back. I've played laser tag a lot in my life, but never been given this much time to play, had such great weapons, or had so much fun. If you're not into laser tag, perhaps you'd like to throw axes, or play pool, or play cornholes on the back patio? My daughter and I went in by ourselves, but by the end of our hour we had made fast friends with another family. As we left, they asked, "Same time next weekend?" I may have to go back home instead next weekend, but let me tell you, the next time I come to town I will be laser tagging at Area 52.

# A Three-Hour Tour

We decided to take a tour of Roswell and met at BrickTown where you can see Lego buildings galore. You can also go on a scavenger hunt there among the Legos. Paul was our guide, and a humorous one at that. The tour normally lasts two hours, but since we asked so many questions he took his time, answered our questions, and spent an extra hour with us. We saw Colonel Blanchard's house, and Air Force Intelligence Officer Jesse Marcel's house—the place where he showed young Jesse Jr. the material from the crash site. We saw the hangar area where they kept the wreckage and, supposedly, the bodies.

Paul took us downtown to show us where the radio building was. He took us many places that I've wanted to see but didn't know where to look. Since 2020, when the tour with Dennis Balthasar ended, Roswell had no tour guide in place, so I was very excited to find that a new guide had started. When you make your Roswell journey, whether by bus, train, plane, or Route 66, make sure you stop by at the visitor center in Roswell, get your picture made with aliens, get your information on the tour, and sign up!

# Lost in Roswell

This year, for the 2023 UFO Festival, I decided to gather up some friends and make it a girl trip. Loretta, Karen, Cindy, and I piled into a tiny—and I do mean tiny—black convertible. We headed out in this little two-door (did I mention it was tiny?) and started the sixteen-hour drive across the country. We left out of Booneville, Mississippi, around midnight, and two days later we pulled into Roswell. We stopped at every Love's gas station in order to save 10 cents a gallon, which seemed to cost us a lot more in the long run because we bought something at almost every store. We made our first night stop in Amarillo, where we stuffed ourselves and drank the amazing beer at The Big Texan. We spray-painted Cadillacs on Route 66, and then headed on to Roswell. As many times as I have been to Roswell, I thought I knew downtown—but now I really know downtown. After the annual alien parade, we decided to walk to see the drone, but we forgot to remember where we parked the little, tiny black convertible. At one o'clock in the morning, we were still searching for that car while wearing alien costumes. That might seem unusual anywhere else, but the police hardly gave us a second glance. Our phones were long dead by this time, but fortunately, after I sat down to ponder our lives and misfortune, I remembered taking a selfie in front of the parade and that meant I remembered where the car was! Only in Roswell do other people stop what they are doing and look for your car with you—and then celebrate with you when you find it! I can also say that Loretta, Karen, and Cindy know all of downtown Roswell now. We bought souvenirs, entered the costume contest, and danced in the streets.

When it was over, we put our human personas back on and headed home along Route 66. This time we visited the Blue Whale in Oklahoma. When I entered the Blue Whale's gift shop I told the attendant, "Today is your lucky day! You have just met your money quota for the day." I have a love of artwork, magnets, and pins. Therefore, I bought their artwork, magnets, and pins. We headed down Route 66 after the gift shop and went to the diner down the street. We met regulars there that talked about how they never expected their town of Catoosa to get so famous. When you go see the Blue Whale, make sure you go to the Highway 66 Diner right down the street, eat one of their amazing Reuben sandwiches, and take a selfie with Marilyn or Frank or many of the others pictured on their walls. The diner will make sure you feel like you are back in the 1950s.

# The Roswell Legend

For those of you who have not heard of the Roswell Crash in 1947, here are the facts as we know them. William Ware "Mack" Brazel, who was a rancher on the Foster ranch, would go and gather weather balloon debris for extra money when he found it here and there. Brazel could take it and get a couple dollars for the scraps. Fact 1: He knew what weather balloons looked like. Moving on, one night, around the Fourth of July, he heard a loud boom in the middle of a terrible storm. The next day, when he was working on the ranch with his neighbor's son, Dee Proctor, he ran across some debris but could not figure out what it could possibly be. It didn't look like anything he had ever seen before. He gathered up some of the wreckage and took it to town to show the sheriff. Sheriff Wilcox called Air Force Intelligence Officer Jesse Marcel. Marcel, Brazel, and Captain Sheridan Cavitt went to examine the debris. Marcel took some of the debris and stopped off at his house to show his son, Jesse Jr., the material. Fact 2: He told his son that he would never see anything like this again, that this material was not of this earth.

The debris was taken to Fort Worth Army Air Field (FWAAF) in Texas. This was when General Ramey took it, told Marcel to leave the room for a moment, and they removed the real stuff and replaced it with some weather balloon debris. When Marcel came back in, they ordered him to take a picture with it. Fact 3: We also know that someone from the Roswell Army Air Field (RAAF) called and talked to mortician Glenn Dennis and asked if he had any child-sized coffins in stock and, if so, could he get more. They later called back and said, "Never mind." He also got another call and was asked how they could stop badly decomposed bodies that had been exposed to weather from deteriorating further.

In the International UFO Museum are affidavits from Glenn Dennis and Roswell citizens who saw and heard things, including their stories of government men who threatened them and told them not to talk. Pappy Henderson, a pilot, flew the bodies to Wright-Patterson Air Force Base near Dayton, Ohio. One very interesting testimony to me was one where a neighbor said Mack Brazel didn't have two nickels to rub together before he left with government men to go to Washington, but when he came back, he was dressed in a suit and driving a new truck. Another odd thing: before Brazel went to Washington, all he could talk about was the crash. When he returned, he refused to say another word about it. He soon packed up and moved to a new town, leaving Roswell for good.

# They Ain't Green

I don't know if aliens crashed near Roswell, but I know something did. I also know it is something the government didn't want to be known. I know it was so big, Mack Brazel was paid to keep quiet. I know it was so big that men in black threatened Roswell citizens. What was the government hiding? Why are people at the United States Air Force facility known as Area 51 so secretive? Why did so many Roswell citizens say what they said they saw? Why did Jesse Marcel Jr. come back to Roswell throughout his life? Why was this place one of the last that he visited? He asked to see his childhood home one more time and got to see it two months before he died. He stood in that kitchen once more, staring at the floor where the unidentified material once lay. Jesse Marcel Jr. was a doctor, a flight surgeon in the army, and made colonel before he died. He had a family. He lived a successful life. His wife Linda said you would never meet a more honest man. His children said he was passionate about UFOs. Why did he believe until the end of his life that this crash was from another world? Why did Mack Brazel refuse to talk about the incident for the rest of his life? The only words he said when an interviewer badgered him was, "They ain't green." How would he know? I wrestle with all the facts and the words of witnesses, of people just like us.

If I cling to a truth all my life, even on my deathbed, would I really protect a lie? The government has been known to lie over and over again. Do I really want to trust the government over hundreds of good people who saw UFO evidence with their own eyes? I know my choice. I also know I have fallen in love with this little town called Roswell. If aliens do return, they will feel at home in this little town that welcomes them. Perhaps a little bit of alien DNA was sprinkled on this town and its people, and it made them nicer than average human beings. Whatever you believe, the incident in 1947 has changed this town for the better. The people at the UFO museum have taken all of the knowledge that they can find about the universe, and they have organized and archived all the information. Spend a day here, perhaps two, or quite a few (like me), and you—perhaps, like me—will not be the same earthling that drove into Roswell.

Milton Keynes UK
Ingram Content Group UK Ltd.
UKHW021528141123
432538UK00011B/102